brother of moon

Ali Fadel

As far as I know, the real horror started in December, that is, in the winter, and by the way, the whole town was covered in snow. Let me introduce myself to you. I'm Jack Smith, and I live in Norn town, in the north of Black Damon.

And by the way, it is one of the coldest places on this planet, where the temperature reaches 72 degrees below zero. This is talk in the winter. In summer, the temperature reaches only twenty degrees!

It was a night. Snow is falling very slowly. I was standing in front of the window with a glass of cold drink in my hand while soft music emanated from the radio subject in the corner of the room.

"Jack... Stop looking out the window. Someone will see you!"

Maybe you are surprised by the words of... But let me tell you, this is a town. Norn town. It is forbidden to drink or sell alcohol, so I was in the barrel of the cannon in case someone saw me drink a glass of cold wine.

I told her:

"Sarah, my love. Don't worry, everything is fine."

But Sarah replied:

Enough sarcasm... You were arrested last week. Don't forget that."

This is my wife. Sarah Kudman... She is thirty-five years old, while I am thirty-six years old. She has blond hair, while I have black hair. She has green eyes, while I have brown eyes. And that's how I described myself and my wife to you.

Any way... Sarah said to me, putting dinner plates on a table:

"Jack, dinner is ready."

She quickly drank the drink and then sat down in front of her, saying,

"The smell of food is indescribable."

Sarah smiled gently, saying,

"Let's eat."

And the moments pass one after another. Like a train loaded with trailers. It passes through a dark tunnel.

Pass one trailer after another. And so on, after half an hour.

I took the dishes off the table, and I sat smoking a cigarette and looking at the ceiling of the room.

But it was only a short moment until my wife came back from the kitchen.

She stood by me. I paid attention to her. I found signs of anxiety painted on her face, and ten years after we were married, I knew what she was thinking. And what do you think?

I told her:

"Sarah ... There's something you're hiding from me, right?"

She started playing with her hair tresses, and this is a movement that, if it indicates tension and anxiety, I went back and asked her:

"What's up? Tell me?"

Sarah sat at a table in front of me, avoiding looking into my eyes.

I told her:

"Is it about procreation?"

FYI Although we have been married for nearly six years, we have not even had a single child. And let me give you an additional piece of information. There were whole nights we fought—me and her—over who was wrong in this matter.

But Jawab surprised me as she said:

"It's about something else, Jack."

And here I felt fear and terror, and my brow began to sweat even though the room was warm, so I said to her quickly:

"Sarah... Tell me. I'm starting to worry."

"I... I'm pregnant!"

My eyes widened to the point that they almost came out of their skull, and I got up from a chair, screaming:

" Really. What are you saying? Is this just a lie? Swear to me."

She got up with tears in her eyes, saying,

"I swear to you. It's a fact."

Here, an adult voice rang out on my device. So, I rushed to him.

A communiqué is coming from Miller's house. Neighbors reported hearing loud fights, and of course, who doesn't know Miller's family consists of a father named Henry and a wife named Mary, and of course they don't have any children?

I got out of my car, then went up the stairs of the house and knocked on the door.

The sky was pitch black. And the snow covers everything around you. You only see a white color, and anyway, the Miller family house had two floors, and like most houses in Norn town,

I opened the door, Mary. I noticed a blue bruise on her right eye. And of course, she raised a bottle of drink at me, saying:

"Go ahead, Jack."

I went inside the house. I found Henry to be a very fat man. And a bald head and eyes like pigs' eyes. As for his clothes, they are almost torn from obesity. How does this pig live?

He was standing near the dining table and looking at me with those piggy-brown eyes.

I put my hand on my gun, saying,

"Henry, you know the rules here. I arrested you three times last week."

He interrupted me as saliva poured out of his mouth, saying,

"I didn't do anything wrong... I love whiskey."

I tried to calm him down, saying:

"Henry, you know the laws."

"Fuck you, Jack."

"Don't force me to do something bad. Get down on your knees and put your hands on your head."

In reality, the issue of shackling this Foolish is a task that is almost as serious. The danger of shackling a pig! If you understand what I mean, this is the body of the full one who almost swore that if he fell on you from above, he would make dough out of you on the ground.

Luckily. Henry was kind-hearted. and understanding. So, I arrested him and took him to an office to put him behind bars.

But the real horror started when he sat in front of me at a table. My colleague at work, Sofia, is also a policewoman.

I was smoking while I was looking out a window outside. She sat in front of me, and she was looking at me.

I told her:

"What's up? Tell me."

And let me tell you about Sofia. She's older than me here. Sofia lived her life here while I was here three months ago. Sofia is 35 years old. And She has red hair. And hazel eyes and let me tell you a secret about it. she always spies on people. Yes, she spies on people. And it's literally. she knows every small and big thing in every house in town.

Sophia told me:

"Have you noticed something strange in a town?"

I looked at her and then blew smoke into the air and said,

"What do you mean?"

Sophia looked into my eyes and said,

"It's been about two months since you've been here."

I interrupted her to correct her information.

"Three months."

"Well. Three months. And you didn't notice anything strange in this town? It's terrifying!"

She blew smoke, saying:

"No, I didn't see anything strange here. Except for the snow and the harsh cold."

"And yet?"

"I didn't see anything suspicious here. People are simple. We are almost isolated from the outside world, and what do you mean by you?"

Sophia breathed audibly as she said,

"People! Haven't you realized anything yet?"

I raised my shoulders indifferently, saying,

"What is wrong with people? If you mean that people behave strangely, then it is up to people, specifically due to the cold weather here. No one can afford this cold."

But her answer shocked me:

"It's not their behavior; it's something worse."

"Something worse?! I don't understand yet."

"Something evil surrounds this town... Something that makes... it makes people sterile."

And while snow hit my car glass, I was coming back from a sheriff's office. I was recalling what Sofia said about the people here. How come I didn't pay attention to this?

Since I set foot, this is a town. Three months ago, I didn't see a single child!! But over time and because of the many events that you meet in your life, it makes you forget a lot of things.

Halfway through, I got a phone call from someone, and I said,

"Jack is with you."

A sharp voice came to me, saying:

"Jack, I'm Michael. I think you need to see this."

"See what?"

"Something strange."

"Where is your location?"

"At the entrance to the forest specifically."

"Well. Wait for me there, and don't move."

"I'm waiting for you."

At the entrance to the woods, I found Michael. Let me tell you about it. He's a hunter who carries a hunting rifle with him and smokes heavily. And he wears black glasses. He has blue eyes and a red beard. He has a scar on his left cheek that he took as a souvenir from one of the wolves that attacked him while he was hunting a wild deer. Luckily for him, His limbs were completely spared, except for the scar representing the wolf's claws.

Michael said as he blew smoke:

"Jack ... How are you?"

"I'd rather get to the heart of a topic, as you know."

Michael laughed and blew smoke: "I'm not surprised at you; you're a capital boy, anyway. There's something I discovered yesterday that you have to see."

The cold winds were hitting my face. And I try hard to follow Michael's steps in the snow. But it's impossible to walk comfortably in this thick snow. When you run over it, it feels like a foot is slipping into a deep world. Very deep!

I said to Michael as I followed him:

"When do we get somewhere?"

And I got an answer quickly:

"We've already arrived."

And in front of us was a dark and wide cave. I looked at Michael, saying,

That's what you wanted to show me. "Cave "

"It's not a cave, sir. but what's inside it?"

Michael lit a red candle to illuminate the place and started to advance me. I was walking with my hand on my gun, just in case. On the other hand, I was carrying a torch.

Michael Lee said:

"Do you smell that, Jack?"

I smelled the atmosphere. Indeed, there is a smell. It has a bad smell, and it is a sulfur smell.

I said to Michael:

"The smell of sulfur. What's wrong with it?"

Michael Lee said:

"There's something you have to see. Come on."

As we walked down the dark corridor of the cave, I heard laughter. I quickly told Michael:

"Do you hear this? The sound of children's laughter!!".

"Nope. Maybe it's just an illusion. Come on."

And here we have reached an exciting part of the story. But Michael turned around and said to me,

"Look at this."

There were strange things on both sides of the cave. Petrified things, or... with the phrase more correct, it was petrified!

And there are, like, wooden poles coming out of the chests of some things.

I said to Michael as I pointed the torch at one of the things:

"What is this a joke?! I traveled every distance to see statues."

"Not statues... Look well!"

Here, I aimed a torch accurately. And I got closer to those things. And I realized that these are not statues:

"That's...".

"Corpses! These are bodies that have been fossilized."

I looked at Michael with my eyes wide.

"This doesn't make sense. Who did this?"

Michael's response:

"I don't know. But there's something strange about these corpses. Look well."

And I realized what Michael was aiming at, and I said:

"These are pegs."

Michael smoked a cigarette, saying:

"To whom do you think they put pegs? in a place of heart."

Because of my lack of knowledge, I asked Michael:

"I don't understand. What do you mean by that?"

Michael blew smoke, saying:

"These are corpses. The correct statement is not human."

"Not human?!"

"This is vampire corpses."

We went back to the entrance of the jungle. I sat in the driver's seat, and Michael approached me and asked me:

"What are you going to do about this cave?"

I looked at him and then said,

"I don't know. Anyway, let's –".

But he quickly interrupted me, saying,

"Have you heard of Dracul's cult, Jack?"

I raised my eyebrows and asked,

"Dracul's sect?! No, I haven't heard anything about it, and I don't want to hear about it."

Michael blew a cigarette and said,

"It is a sect that worships an evil entity. It is said that he dwells on the moon! and scary about the subject that they are among us here... In this damn town."

She smiled at Michael, saying,

"And where is the problem with that? Some people want to worship a God of their own."

"A real problem. are the gossip that spreads about them."

"What kind of gossip, Michael?"

"They are said to be the reason why all the people in this town are sterile!!".

I was surprised by Michael's answer, and I told him:

"You know about it?"

"The only person who doesn't know is you, Jack. And I'm not surprised that you didn't pay attention to this because you're a new person in town."

"Well... The time for talking is over. If anything happens, call me."

"Concept."

I sat on a bed reading a horror novel called (The Beast). While Sarah was lying next to me.

I realized Sara was looking at me with her green eyes. I told her:

"What's up?"

"Did you know? I had a strong headache, so I went to Ludwig's family house to ask them for a headache remedy."

I interrupted her as I looked at the pages of the novel.

"Why did you go? There are medicines in the bathroom."

"They're all out of it. I have a severe headache these days."

And here a moment of silence came. So, I cut it off, saying,

"And what happened after you went to Charles's house?"

I got to know them. Rebecca's wife called me; she was a nice person, and her husband, Charles, was a dark man. I couldn't leave their house quickly. She invited me to have a cake.

I interrupted her, and I was annoyed by all this nonsense.

"Go to sleep."

"Stop reading. I'm talking to you, Jack."

I was more annoyed, but I decided to leave a novel, and then I looked at her green eyes, saying:

"Well... Let me tell you. You know me. If there's something important, get it into the heart of a topic without twisting and turning."

"Don't be mad at me, Jack. I was trying to draw details for you."

Please. Sarah. "Tell me something I want to hear."

Here, Sarah told me something strange:

"Did you know that they can't have children? It's been thirty years since they got married, and they didn't have any children."

And here I wanted to hear more information from her, so I said:

"Did you see anything strange or suspicious in their house?"

"Yes. Three strange things."

And here my eyes widened, and I asked her, saying:

"Three things? What do you mean?"

Sarah replied:

"Like, there aren't any mirrors in their house."

And here my eyes widened, and I asked her, saying:

"Three things? What do you mean by you?"

Sarah replied:

"Like there is no mirror in their house!"

I raised my eyebrows, asking:

"Unbelievable! A whole house without a mirror?"

Sarah nodded in agreement.

I moderated my sitting and then put my hand on my chin as I asked her:

"What's next?"

Sarah moderated as well and replied:

"And the second thing... They're all weird skin colors."

Here I realized what she was aiming for, and I said to her:

"Their skin color is pale, isn't it?"

Sarah raised her eyebrows in apparent stupidity and said,

"Yes. How do you know that?".

"It doesn't matter. Tell me the third thing you saw."

Here, Sarah replied:

"They don't have any crosses, and that's weird?"

Here I wondered:

"Maybe they're atheists for this reason."

Sarah interrupted me, saying:

"I asked a husband, and he told me they were Christians."

Here, I could see ice gathering on the transparent window glass. And a moment of silence came when I was thinking about myself. The bodies that I saw this morning in a cave with Michael. Don't leave my mind. Carcasses of vampires.

That's the only place where vampires and werewolves live. Horror stories

As far as we know, it doesn't happen in real life.

And so, I told Sarah to go to sleep. And I turned off the lamp so that the room would be dark.

"Jaaaaaak!." The sound of a scream resounded, which took me from a dream world to reality. I got up from bed and saw Sarah missing, so I pulled a staircase next to me, took a gun, and went down from the staircase to the first floor.

Sarah! Sarah!"

"Jack, Jack, I'm here!"

It was a voice coming from a kitchen, so I went to it, and here I saw Sarah kneeling on the ground crying while a man was wearing a black mask with cleft eyes and a mouth like those of bank robbers.

He was putting his gun on Sarah's head, equipped. I raised my gun at him and said in a threatening tone:

"Leave Sarah! And put down your weapon."

The man looked at me and then said in a very quiet voice:

"I think you see the fate of what awaits your wife if you don't let go of your gun."

I couldn't think of anything at that time. Then I dropped a gun on the ground.

"Throw it away."

The man said it quietly as if he had carried out operations like these dozens of times before.

I threw my gun and hit one of the legs of a table, then I got up and said,

"Who are you? And what do you want?"

The man said quietly:

"They paid me to bring your wife to them."

I raised my eyebrows, saying:

"They paid? Who are they?"

"It's none of your business."

Here I asked the man an important question:

"I'm not a murderer, right?"

The man's gaze was as cold as frost, and a man answered me:

"Right. I told you, they paid me to bring your wife."

And here the man added:

"You will drink this drink!"

And with his left hand, he threw me a small bottle of syrup. It's about the size of a finger. He told me with a threatening tone:

"Drink it. Not poison."

"I get it. It contains a powerful anesthetic, right?"

"You have some intelligence now drinks it."

I smiled and said,

"What if I refuse it?"

The man looked at Sarah kneeling under his legs and said,

"You know what's going to happen to her."

"They told you to bring her alive, not dead."

That's when I heard the man's breathing. I probably made him angry with my last phrase.

The man raised his gun in the direction and said,

"They told me to bring it alive, but you have a choice to decide your destiny; either drink it or you die."

Here, I have no choice anymore. This is a man who is not joking. I opened a bottle and then smelled it, and then a man said:

"Drink it, come on."

I took a dose of it. The man became angry, saying,

"Drink it all at once."

I did what I was asked to do. For a few seconds, I didn't feel anything, but I was surprised after that I fell to the ground and everything around me started spinning, and then the darkness covered everything.

I woke up and found myself on the wooden kitchen floor. I got up quickly and found my gun near a table, so I took it and dressed in a sheriff's uniform. Then I called my police colleagues, and police patrols started searching everywhere, and I was with them.

Finally ... It's useless; it's completely gone from the town. And here I remembered something. What did the kidnapper mean?

Is there anyone who hates me in his town? I don't know if we excluded, of course, neighbors. I don't think neighbors kidnap your wife just because they hate you.

Dracul's sect... She is the one who paid him.

Is there a common denominator between the Dracule cult and the kidnapper? Is it possible that a sect asked to kidnap my wife? But why? What is the motive behind that?

I sat in the kitchen with a gun in front of me. Sophia sat next to me, trying to calm me down.

"We'll find her, Jack."

"Sofia... Me- I'm fine. Thank you."

Sofia got up, said goodbye, and sat alone in a house. Where did it disappear? My wife, Sara, what are you doing now?

You see her crying in return for waiting for her unknown fate. I'll find you, Sara. Trust me...

In the Black Swan Pub. I sat on one of the benches, sipping a glass of wine, to calm down my fear for my beloved wife.

It was an empty pub except for Harold, who is my bartender, of course. A big, black-skinned, bald man.

"You heard what happened, Jack. I'm sorry."

I drank a cup inside my hollow.

And here, a crazy idea came to mind.

And I said to Harold:

"Never mind. But I want to know one thing from you. Will you allow me?"

Harold put a towel on his right shoulder like all bartenders do in bars and then said:

"Go ahead."

Here, I told him the following:

"Do you know anything about the Dracule sect?"

I noticed that his pupils dilated for a few seconds and then tried to lie to me, saying:

"No, sir, I know nothing about them."

"Do you have children, Harold?"

"No, sir."

"Good. Now tell me about a sect, and don't try to lie to me."

Sweat began to pour from his black forehead, and he tried more than once to avoid looking into my eyes. Here I used a threatening technique, saying:

"You know lying to the police is a crime punishable by law. Either tell me everything you know about these or... I can take you to the office, and there you will talk."

"I... I can't speak, Jack."

Here I raised my gun in his face, and he stepped back and hit his back against the shelves of cups, and some of them fell and broke on the ground.

He raised his hands in front of his face, saying,

"Please don't kill me."

"This is an option that depends on you!".

"I'll tell you... I'll tell you everything I know. Don't tell me, please!"

You might be surprised by my doing this. But it's a very normal act for me. He refused to tell me, so he forced me to use my threat. Maybe you're wondering about me. Are you a cop? How do you do that?

I'll tell you then. By closing your mouth and getting away from my face.

"Well... Tell me everything you know about them, and no lies, Harold."

"Present.".

I didn't put down my gun, but I held it in front of his face to force him to confess more. He told me:

"They are an evil sect... A sect that controls everything and their being lies in the dreaded moon."

"I want their names right away."

"I don't know much about them, but one day... Scar. That drunken boy, He talked about a cult"

"Scar Tyler?"

"Yes, yes."

"Are you sure that's true?"

"I swear by my wife's life."

"Well... Harold. Are you going to file a complaint against me?"

"No, sir."

"Well. Good expense, please."

"For free, I don't want anything."

Here, I smiled as I got up, but I put on a twenty-dollar bill, and before I went out, I told him:

"Keep the rest."

Scar Taylor lived in a moving trailer on the outskirts of town. And he is a man in his thirties, unmarried. He has black hair and black eyes, and I don't forget the most important note that he has a tattoo on his whole body, as he is one of the characters that love to draw silly tattoos.

Trailer door knocked:

"Scar Taylor? I'm Jack Smith. Sheriff. Open the door."

I got a voice from inside the trailer:

"Who? What do you want?"

Here, I was very angry:

"Open the damn door, or I'll smash it."

Scar Taylor opened the door. So I went inside quickly, and let me tell you that this is a man who lives in chaos. His clothes are everywhere.

Pictures of naked women fill every spot of his trailer. And let me tell you that I found a blonde-haired prostitute sitting on top of a bed, and I told her:

"Leave immediately."

A prostitute got up and got dressed, and then, before leaving, she said goodbye to Scar, saying:

"Goodbye, darling."

"Goodbye".

Here is what Scar Taylor told me:

"What's the matter, Sheriff?"

But my answer to him was a strong punch with the heel of my gun against his long nose. We'll have fun, rat...

Here is what Scar Taylor told me:

"What's the matter, Sheriff?"

But my answer to him was a strong punch with the heel of my gun against his long nose. So he fell to the ground on a trailer. Blood was pouring out of his nose as he said,

"Why did you hit me?".

"Shut your mouth."

I immediately put my gun on his head as I told him:

"You have two choices: either you die or you live. Choose?"

The features of terror began to sculpt a white face, which encouraged me to continue in the role of the ruthless criminal.

"Please don't kill me."

Why do they always say this silly sentence, whether in movies or stories? If someone wanted to kill someone else, it would be impossible to give you a chance to even breathe! Maybe in cases of revenge, for example. Maybe you are given some moments to savor lust as revenge, but this is another topic.

I pressed the gun to his head more and said,

"I told you to choose."

"R... Live.. I want to live."

Here I told him:

"Get up quickly."

So Scar got up, holding his nose, which was pouring blood from my strong blow, and I pointed to the bed where a prostitute was sleeping on top of it and said:

"Sit on a bed."

So Scar sat down and almost swore that his body was trembling like a child. To this degree of death.

I told him, still pointing a gun at him:

"You told me you wanted to live... Fair enough.. This is a suitable option. Tell me where my wife is."

"Jack, I'm --.".

"You don't know where it is, right?"

Scar lowered his gaze to the ground and said,

"Yes. I don't know."

"Well. This is your first lie."

And I pulled out the gun to prepare for the killing.

Scar got up from the bed and said,

"I swear a-... Know... I don't know... I -".

"This question determines your life. But sit down first."

Scar sat down again; sweat was wetting his chest and forehead, and he almost swore he almost wet his white pants.

I told him:

"You're a member of the Dracule sect, right?"

Scar said to me:

"No. What are you saying, man? I don't know who you're talking about."

That's where a volcano of anger started to rise. Out of my coat pocket, I took out the muffler nozzle. And I prepared a silencer with a gun.

Scar got up and said,

"Yes. I'm one of them. I'm one of them; don't shoot."

What do you expect you to do to him? No, I wouldn't kill him, if that's your idea. Three faint bullets were fired because of a silencer. Next to Scar on a bed, three bullets pierced the bed cover.

That's when I saw Paul covering Scar's underpants. He on himself...

I pointed the gun at his face and said,

"Your last chance. Talk about everything that belongs to a sect, or I'll empty a bullet magazine in your skull."

"I swear I'll talk, but don't kill me."

And he raised his hands, trying to make it appear not to be dangerous.

"Let's talk fast."

"Dracul's sect... You're trying to save the city from a monster. For this, they need to kill a pregnant woman to extract the baby from her womb for the sake of (the brother of the moon)."

I was disgusted to hear the last words and said:

"What? Do you want me to blow your head off?"

"I swear to you in my mother's grave. It's true, sir."

"Monster? A sect trying to save a town from a monster!"

"Sir, you don't understand the meaning very well. The monster is one of the members of a sect. The monster is controlled by (the brother of the moon). The entity that rules from the moon, and to secure the evil of this monster, they have to kill a pregnant woman every year for this operation."

"Nonsense. I don't believe you, pig."

"I swore to you at my mother's grave. I'm not lying. The Dracule sect worships... One of the gods Eldrich worships is Brother of the Moon, who was detained inside the moon itself."

"Goddess Eldrich?! Who the hell are they?"

Scar swallowed and then said,

"An evil cosmic god. Beings coming from the depths of the dark universe. No human mind can see them or imagine how powerful they are."

"Great, from monsters to the world of babies. Very great. Of course, I will not imprison you because it is not suitable for the insane."

Here, a moment of silence came between us. And somehow, I remembered bodies in a cave, and I said,

"Do you know the secret of corpses in that cave in a black forest? Are they vampires?"

Scar's eyes widened, and then he said cautiously:

"Vampires?! No, they are. They were members of the sect in the past."

"I didn't understand; explain more."

"These have received the blessing of the great (brother of the moon), so they were stoned on both sides of the cave to prepare for the coming of He."

"Who?"

"Brother of the Moon".

That's where I lowered my gun and Scar breathed in happiness, but... I decided not to leave him for a moment, so I raised my gun again in his face, and suddenly I erected with signs of fear still on him:

"you said there was a monster! Fair enough... What kind of monster are you talking about?"

No one knows what he looks like. And as far as I know, everyone who saw a monster never saw light again!

Did you know? He's an idiot. He uses a cheap method, as in some horror stories.

I told him:

"The last question is: Where is my wife?"

"Believe me, I don't know where it is. But often a ritual is held in a cave."

"Vampire cave?"

"Yes. It is there where you will—and swallow his throat—sacrifice your wife to extinguish the raging spirit of the beast."

There was a question knocking on my head, and I said:

"you told me that a sect owns the beast and that the beast is one of them. Fair enough... Why don't they kill a monster?"

"We can't. A monster was a curse from the brother of the moon, and even if you kill the beast, the curse will be transmitted to a member of a sect. Even if all members of a sect die, a curse will be associated with their grandchildren or children."

Here I asked a question:

"Who is the head of the sect? Where does the sect of the beast hide?"

"We don't know each other. Our meetings are held in a cave around fires. And let me show you something so you can believe me."

Here is the most prominent scar tongue out of his mouth. And here I saw a blue sign that looks like a satanic star that you see in cheap horror movies...

"What is this?"

It's damn. Of course, I don't mean ".

"Wait! I don't understand. Are you trying to say that a monster is a human?! ."

"Exactly... At midnight, you will resist the ritual of sacrificing your wife. And at that moment, you will only have two options."

I raised my eyebrows and said, wondering:

"Two options? Is that a threat, Scar? And I moved my gun to scare him a little.

But Scarr responded:

"Either you save a town from a monster but sacrifice your wife and child... Or save your wife, but the consequences will be dire."

"What do you mean by serious consequences?"

"If you save your wife, you will unleash the beast because the seal will weaken at that moment, and then you will free a monster from a pot... And of course, you know what he's going to do with the town."

"The strongest monsters can't face bullets."

Scar wiped the sweat from his forehead, saying,

"You don't understand, sir. I'll tell you something clearer. You currently own the fate of the town in your hands. Either you sacrifice your wife to save a town or you save your wife—assuming you can save her—but you will shoot a monster at a town of cucumbers with your own hands, sir."

I approached Scar and put my gun on his forehead, then lowered my head to a low level, looked into his brown eyes, and said,

"The human race or my wife... I will choose my wife and let the human race go to hell."

Silence.

I turned to get out, but I stood at the door and looked at Scar, saying,

"Two things... Run away from his town immediately. Second, don't try to file any complaint against me, Clear?".

"Clear, sir."

"Good"

At midnight

I parked my car at the entrance to the forest with two police cars in each car. There are two people because the damn town of Norn has only four cops!... Even if you ask for support from Capital, it's going to take a while. About a week at best, especially with this very cold atmosphere.

I got out of the car carrying a gun. And she smoked a cigarette quickly while Tamari prepared her gun. And Sofia too.

Sophia told me:

"Are you sure of what I said?"

"Yes. Scar told me every detail about a monster. And the bodies of the stranger. And the gods are universal. Etc... And from this nonsense, I knew that there was a sect that intended to sacrifice my wife for the sake of a God who would dwell on the moon!!."

Then I said to the team out loud:

"Ready?"

Everyone replied, "Yes, Hazrat Bailiff.".

"Let's go, guys."

As we walked in the snow with our shoes, a shadow emerged from behind trees.

"Stop where you are!" and everyone raised their weapons.

"Woo. Calm down, guys. That's me."

I looked at his black glasses and said,

"Michael, what are you doing here?"

"Nothing just hunted a deer or a rabbit."

And of course, he was carrying a sniper rifle with him. Raising his eyebrows, Michael asked:

"Is there a problem, Commissioner?"

"Nothing. I want you to go home. Clear?"

"Of course. Is there a particular problem?."

Sophia said:

"It's none of your business. Leave immediately."

It's in Sophia's nature that she talks strictly to everyone. And this was so annoying to everyone he met that, as far as I knew, she was the second most hated figure in a town... You might be wondering about the center of

The first one, yes, gentlemen, is Mayor Harry.

Michael is out of our way. And of course, the night had come, carrying darkness everywhere, and we could not light flashlights because this is something that exposes us. And so on, after a while. We arrived at a cave, and here we hid behind a giant brawl. In front of us, Sarah was crying as she was tied to a wooden pole, and around her were about twenty people wearing white masks and white cloaks as well.

I don't know why Scar's voice came to mind, saying:

"A sect that is not evil. You're trying to calm the beast by sacrificing your wife."

Thoughts flicked from my head, and Mary approached as she said:

"What are we going to do?"

"Go east and then get distracted, and Sam and I will save Sarah."

"Why don't we just go out to them?" Sam said it with obvious stupidity.

And here I forgot to tell you... Sam, the second man after me. Excuse me; I forgot to introduce you to him.

Sam said:

"Look at them. These are fanatic religious sects. If you go out, you'll only see monsters that want to tear apart."

Sophia said:

"Are we moving forward with a plan now?"

"Come on."

Two girls moved with their guns to the east while Sam and I waited for a suitable moment. But there's Sara's imam. Someone was wearing a cloak. A blue cloak is different from all the white cloaks worn by everyone around him; this is their leader, without a doubt.

but for a few seconds. A person took down an abaya from his body to appear naked, and it turned out that this, or, let's say, this... Girl ... How do you know? She has a long braid. And you rarely find a man with a long braid if he is only from Viking...

And the blue moon appeared in the sky and shined its light on the trees. Earth... The leaves of a tree

Then, for seconds, I saw in front of us a scene, because of which my mind almost stopped.

The girl started kneeling as if she were in pain from something, and suddenly a long tail protruded from above her buttocks, and black hair began to grow all over her body, and her legs turned into goat legs.

And her chest gained clear muscles. As for her head, it turned into a bull's head. With horns and a snout that blows white smoke.

I felt terrified, mixed with fear, and my weapon fell on the ice against my will.

Sam said to me, his eyes almost coming out of their quarries in shock:

"What's that?!"

She replied after I lifted my gun: "Hang on, man."

My wife, Sarah, started screaming as she saw the monster approaching her. While all the sects read like poetic hymns, I think it's a kind of prayer or begging. Or something I don't know anything about.

I looked at Tamari and Sofia and gave a signal.

And the battle began.

The two girls came out from behind trees, screaming:

"Don't move. Police are surrounding a place."

But the beast turned to them and moved to her. From the top of the hill, me and Sam see in front of me a group of men from a sect. Of course, I did not hesitate for a single moment, so I fired a barrage of bullets from my pistol.

A bullet penetrated someone's head and detonated him like a children's balloon.

Another person came with a knife. I thought these were men who didn't carry weapons. But I was wrong...

I shot the man in the stomach. The man rushed back a few meters to fall with his stomach pierced.

Sam also did not hesitate. So, he was shooting left and right.

Sam shouted after blowing someone's head off:

What are you waiting for? Save your wife!

I ran, and I was shooting here and there. To everyone who stands in front of me, no mercy. They are the ones who wanted that. So, they take responsibility.

I went up the podium. And here I saw my wife's face and tears in her eyes.

"Jack".

" Sarah. I came to save you. Don't worry, honey."

And I cut the ropes with the knife I carry. Then she and I ran. I shouted at Sam:

Come on, Sam."

Sam shot one of them, and then we fled a place after we committed a real massacre. These are evil people.

Sam, I, and my wife were running. Sam said to me:

"Sofia and Tamari!."

She replied to him:

"Don't worry, they killed the monster and fled like us."

But we heard Sophia screaming as she said:

"Help me!"

We stopped suddenly and looked back. Sofia was limping, and blood was covering her clothes.

And here we saw radiant red eyes behind Sofia.

For a second, I couldn't believe what he saw.

A monster caught Sofia. by her hair and lifted her in the air as she struggled to let her go.

Then the monster grabbed her by one of her feet. To tear it in half like a piece of paper.

Sam shouted as he fired his gun:

"Sofia... no, no."

I didn't hesitate for a moment. Sarah and I continued our way out of the woods.

Outside, our cars were parked. We rode in a car here. Sam's head hit the glass of our car and then fell into the snow.

I moved the car and then started driving at its speed.

And I look sometimes behind me and sometimes in front of me.

Sarah said in tears:

"I'm scared. We're going to die."

"No, sweetheart. I exist Nothing will happen to you, believe me."

I was expecting the monster to appear at any moment for.

In front of us or behind us. Or even if it's on top of the car.

But we got to his town. And then we entered our house...

I told her:

"Pack all your stuff. We're leaving this town."

I looked through the glass. And here I saw someone running with something in his hand. And for a few seconds, I avoided the window.

Something pierced the window to start burning. Miltov ... I took off my jacket and tried to put out the fire. But gas was faster than me.

Sarah came down screaming, and I told her:

"The back door. Quickly."

She and I ran. Then we opened the door and found in front of us a man carrying a racket.

Of course, he was one of the members of a sect.

It blew his head off with one bullet, and he fell dead.

We ran towards the car. Sons of. They ripped the tires off the four cars. Now what did he do?

Sarah told me:

"What do we do?"

I told her:

"I have a plan."

And in my car, there was a box with four grenades in it. So, I took out two of them and told her:

"Carry this!"

"I've gone crazy."

"Just carry it!"

Sarah picked up two of them, and then we ran through the streets of town. On the way, I found the four from a sect. And they didn't wear masks.

One of them, who had a red beard, said,

"You are destroying a town... The beast will not calm down."

And here the monster jumped on the roof of one of the houses next to us, and we heard a raging bellow sound as it jumped in our direction.

We ran back while she looked behind me.

I found a monster killing two of the sect's men while the other two were trying to kill the monster.

Everywhere around us.

Screams were getting louder. The town's houses started burning suddenly. You see smoke rising from the gray clouds.

While the blue moon had risen high and prominent amid the gray clouds.

We entered one of the houses and then closed the door behind us. Fortunately, it was an empty house. Maybe its inhabitants migrated a few moments ago.

I was in front of the door with my gun raised and my hands shaking. Not out of fear, of course, but from extreme tiredness and fatigue.

And here Sarah said to me:

"What are we going to do? The town is being destroyed!"

Told:

"Don't worry, honey, everything will be fine."

We're third. Me, her, and We know that the sentence that was said above...

Just a white lie: things have always been going against their usual course.

Here, we heard knocks on the door. It's as if someone hit the door with an axe.

She shouted out loud:

"you sons of--."

Of course...

Strong knocks continued on the door, especially after they heard my screams. And here, I heard the sound of glass breaking from behind us.

I turned around, and Sarah stepped back behind me.

I saw a man wearing a mask, holding a cleaver in his right hand, running towards me. I shot him. It hit his right leg. So he fell to the ground and started to groan from pain and the blood that started to cover the floor.

I went forward toward him, and I tightened my grip on my gun.

The man with a mask raised his left hand as he said:

"Mercy".

"No mercy to you."

And a bullet was fired into his head. This is a true mercy.

And all of a sudden, We heard the sound of the door being smashed behind us. Sarah screamed as she stepped back from the door.

So I saw

The axe head is trying to smash the door.

"Go to the second floor."

Sarah went up to the second floor. While I stood waiting for the door to break down,

The man continued to smash the door.

But I stepped through the door. And then, with my left hand, I opened it.

and for a few seconds. A man was raising his axe, intending to strike the door that I opened.

I raised my gun, and a bullet came out faster than an axe.

His head exploded and fell on the steps of the house. Out ...

Fires were starting to take a dangerous turn. The men of the sect were masked, wreaking havoc and destruction here and there.

And the beast is absent; we don't know where it is.

Houses are looted and burned. Cars break the men of a sect kill the townspeople sounds scream everywhere

I closed the door quickly, and I saw three men coming.

This door won't last long.

I threw a pistol. After he finished bullets, I filled a new store. The first man opened the door, and I was greeted by a bullet. So, he fell dead on the ground, but two

Hide beside the door.

Someone said to me:

"Surrender, Jack. The town was destroyed because of you."

Another man said:

"You preferred your wife to a town. What a selfish person you are."

One of them said:

"Look at the blue moon; it's really beautiful!!".

And then I only saw Miltov throwing in my direction.

I backed down in the last seconds.

Meletov fell to the ground, and fire spread everywhere at hellish speed.

Two men ran away.

I tried to go up to the second floor, but the fire was faster than me. She cried out loudly:

Sarah! Sarah! Don't come down."

Sarah's voice came from the top of the floor:

"Jack... Fire!".

"Don't be afraid, dear. Look for a window. About a director Come on."

And I turned to get out from behind the house through the door behind me, overlooking a small garden with a swing and green grass covered with thick white snow.

I looked at the top of the house. I saw a window and shouted:

"Sarah... Sarah."

for a few seconds. Sarah was mostly looking for an exit, and she found the window. But there's a real problem. How are you going to do it?

Sarah opened a window and said,

"How do I get off?!"

My mind was unable to imagine any plan at that moment, so I said to her:

"Jump. Jump out of a window."

"Have you gone crazy? I'm pregnant."

And here I saw nothing but a giant black shadow that fell from the sky on a roof.

My eyes widened as I looked at the beast. A bull's head, a body covered with muscles, a tail that hangs, and a goat's legs, but its height, as I said, is about two and a half meters.

I raised my gun and fired three bullets quickly.

The bullets hit the body of the beast, but they did not affect it, as if they were balls of snow.

What did the monster do at that moment?

It was one of the very hard moments for me. The monster entered from the roof above the house to the inside of the room, and here I saw Sarah being pulled away from a window.

She shouted out loud:

"Sarah... No."

And here, the monster threw something out of my window. He fell at my feet. And when I looked closely...

I only found Sara's upper body.

Here, tears came down, and I went crazy. And she cried:

"Sarah no."

And I knelt on the snow as I hugged Sara's upper body.

And here, the beast threw her underbody at me.

Then he jumped out of a window to land on me.

I heard the sound of his bellows as he approached. And I smelled a bad smell, like a strong sulfur smell, and the black hair that covered his thighs.

She left Sarah's body and looked into his red eyes.

"Son of a... I killed her!"

snarling a monster and punching me hard, I flew a distance of ten meters.

After it hit the wooden fence that surrounds the house.

I got up on the ice and started to spit blood out of my mouth.

And I'm looking at him. He advances with steps that leave a goat's hoof's mark on the snow.

This is a good moment. I remembered what to keep.

The monster stood on top of my head and then roared as he pressed his leg on my back.

I screamed in pain as I felt a force that was almost tearing my back apart.

And here I rolled over after he lifted his leg from my back.

I looked into his eyes and said,

"Goodbye, son of a--."

Here, his eyes came down red from my eyes to look at what I was holding in my hand.

It was a bomb.

Here, I felt nothing but a white light, and then darkness covered everything.

Done.